Hammer ✠ Cross

DELUXE CORE RULEBOOK

A Micro Chapbook RPG Rulebook
of Gothic Vampire Horror
Designed by Noah Patterson

Hammer

Cross

Find us on DriveThru RPG!

STOP!

DON'T BUY THIS BOOK!
At least, not yet.

The basic rules for the Micro Chapbook RPG system can be downloaded for FREE in any Micro Chapbook through DriveThruRPG.com. Each stand alone Chapbook includes the complete rules for you to play the game. (I highly recommend Manor of Blood if you're interested in a simple vampire game).

With that in mind, this Deluxe Edition Core Rulebook also contains all the rules you need to play the game plus a few additions. This core book is focused on gothic horror and therefore adds new rules special to vampires and vampire hunting.

This book is completely compatible with ANY and ALL Chapbook Scenarios. In fact, this book includes the system's very first mini campaign--featuring multiple dungeon scenarios within it. After that you can download any number of the free products in the Micro Chapbook line for further scenarios and adventures.

ART CREDITS:

Cover Art: © 2015 Dean Spencer, used with permission. All rights reserved.
Section 1.0 Art: Jose Cardona
Section 9.0 Art: Publisher's Choice Quality Stock Aart © Rick Hershey / Fat Goblin Games
Section 10.0 Art: Publisher's Choice Quality Stock Aart © Rick Hershey / Fat Goblin Games
Section 11.0 Art: Patrick E. Pullen
Section 12.0 Art: Patrick E. Pullen
Section 13.0 Art: Patrick E. Pullen
Section 14.0 Art: Robert Martin
Section 14.1 Art: Robert Martin
Section 15.0 Art: Jesus Duran
Section 16.0 Art: Patrick E. Pullen
Section 17.0 Art: Patrick E. Pullen
Section 18.0 Art: Robert Martin
Section 18.1 Art: Robert Martin
Section 20.0 Art: Publisher's Choice Quality Stock Aart © Rick Hershey / Fat Goblin Games
Section 21.0 Art: Publisher's Choice Quality Stock Aart © Rick Hershey / Fat Goblin Games
Section 22.0 Art: Pablo Marcos
Section 23.0 Art: Jose Cardona
Section 24.0 Art: Patrick E. Pullen
Section 25.14 Art: Patrick E. Pullen
Section 26.0 Art: Robert Martin
Section 27.0 Art: Jesus Duran

Contents

Section 1.0

What is a Hammer + Cross?

Hammer + Cross is a simple dungeon crawling roleplaying game of Gothic Vampire Horror that can be played solo or with a traditional GM (The Lord of Night) if you so wish. It is the second Deluxe Core Rulebooks for The Micro Chapbook RPG system and is compatible with all source books, scenarios, and adventures in that system. You can play the basic game by downloading any of the FREE Chapbooks in the system.

The main game focuses on solitaire gameplay, starring a single vampire hunter out against the forces of darkness. It uses randomly generated dungeon scenarios to make each game session a little different. This book includes a premade mini-campaign: Vengeance on Volkoria Village.

Hammer + Cross is set in an 1890s European inspired fantasy world. However, this version of 1890s Europe has a more horrific and fantastical nature about it. Vampires are real, as are many other demonic and evil minions of the night.

The game is a tribute to gothic horror films and literature—most specifically the Hammer Horror Films. The game is strongly impacted and attuned to the gothic and foreboding themes, atmosphere, and mood of those films.

For some inspiration and insight into the vibe we're going for here, I highly recommend watching some of the following films:

> The Revenge of Frankenstein (1958)
> The Evil of Frankenstein (1964)
> Frankenstein Created Woman (1967)
> Frankenstein Must Be Destroyed (1969)
> The Horror of Frankenstein (1970)
> Frankenstein and the Monster from Hell (1973)
> The Brides of Dracula (1960)
> Dracula: Prince of Darkness (1966)
> Dracula Has Risen from the Grave (1968)
> Taste the Blood of Dracula (1970)

Scars of Dracula (1970)
The Kiss of the Vampire (1963)
Vampire Circus (1971)
Captain Kronos, Vampire Hunter (1974)
The Vampire Lovers (1970)
Lust for a Vampire (1971)
Twins of Evil (1971)
The Hound of the Baskervilles (1959)
The Two Faces of Dr. Jekyll (1960)
The Curse of the Werewolf (1961)
The Phantom of the Opera (1962)
The Gorgon (1964)
The Witches (1966)
The Plague of the Zombies (1966)
The Reptile (1966)
The Devil Rides Out (1968)
Countess Dracula (1971)
Hands of the Ripper (1971)

Section 2.0

What Do I Need to Play?

In order to play Hammer + Cross you will need to gather the following easy-to-find items:

2 six-sided dice
A sheet or notepad of graph paper (or a game mat with a grid)
A Character Sheet (or note paper)
A pencil with a good eraser
These rules or any stand alone chapbook scenario.
Extra scenarios and modules (optional).
Micro Chapbook RPG game supplements (optional).

Section 3.0

Gameplay Basics

During gameplay, you almost always roll 1D6, trying to score equal to or LOWER than your stat score. If your character is proficient in the stat being tested, roll 2 dice and take the better result of the 2. 1 always succeeds. 6 always fails. This mechanic is used for all tasks including attacking, avoiding traps, unlocking doors, and most everything else. The only time this is different is when you roll for damage (either when dealing weapon damage or taking damage from a monster or trap). Some damage scores may ask you to roll 1D3. When you see 1D3 it means you roll a single D6 and half the result rounding up. When you need to roll 1D2, roll 1 die. Odds are 1, evens are 2.

Section 4.0

Character Creation

Character creation is completed in 5 very simple steps:

1. Determine The 4 Stat Scores.
2. Choose a Character Class.
3. Choose a Character Order.
4. Determine Your Starting Health, Willpower, and Faith.
5. Roll for Pounds (£) and Purchase Items.

Each step is explained in further detail in the following sections.

Section 5.0

Character Stats

Your character has 4 main statistics:

Strength (ST): Used for melee attacks and breaking down doors.

Dexterity (DE): Used for ranged attacks and avoiding some traps.

Wits (WI): Used for disarming traps and picking locks.

Charisma (CH): Used for increasing your Willpower and showing your bravery.

During character creation you are granted 7 points to assign between the 4 stats as you see fit (9 for an easier game). No stat can have a score lower than 1 or higher than 4 during this step, but these may be altered later on.

Section 6.0

Character Classes

There are 4 Character Classes to Choose From. Each one will make you proficient in one stat.

Soldier: Soldiers are adept at hand to hand combat and ST based tests. They are proficient in Strength.

Hunter: Hunters are adept at long range combat and DE based tests. They are proficient in Dexterity.

Nurse/Doctor: Nurses/Doctors are adept at healing, puzzle solving, and WI based tests. They are proficient in Wits.

Priest/Nun: Priests and Nuns are adept at holding onto their Willpower and Bravery. They are proficient in Charisma.

Section 6.1

Crafting Your Own Class

If none of the given classes appeal to you, feel free to craft one of your own!

To do this is simple. Think of any class you'd want to play as. What is their background, history, and skills? What proficiency would they have?

Write in the class name and the Stat Proficiency on your sheet.

Section 7.0

Character Order

There are 4 Character Orders to Choose From. Each one will grant you a +1 bonus in one stat. Orders replace Race in this game.

Order of the Hammer: Members of this Order specialize in the art of killing. They recieve +1 in Strength.

Order of the Dagger: Members of this Order specialize in subterfuge. They recieve +1 in Dexterity.

Order of the Cross: Members of this Order specialize in study and occult knowledge. They recieve +1 in Wits.

Order of the Sun: Members of this Order specialize in bravery and confidence in the face of evil. They recieve +1 in Charisma.

Section 7.1

Crafting Your Own Order

If none of the given orders appeal to you, feel free to craft one of your own! An Order is a secret organization with a special group of people working together to hunt and slay evil. To create an Order is simple. Think of any Order you'd want to play as. What is the Order's history? Why were they founded? What is their goal? What stat bonus would they have? Write in the Order name and the Stat bonus on your sheet.

Section 8.0

Death, Will, and Faith

Your Health, Willpower, and Faith are determined by your current stats.

Health: Your health is the total sum of your Strength + Dexterity + 20 (+10 for a challenge).

Willpower: Your will is the total sum of your Wits + Charisma + 20 (+10 for a challenge).

Faith: Your Faith (a new concept to this version of the game system) is the total sum of your Wits + 20 (+ 25 if you're a Priest/Nun).

Section 9.0

Weapons

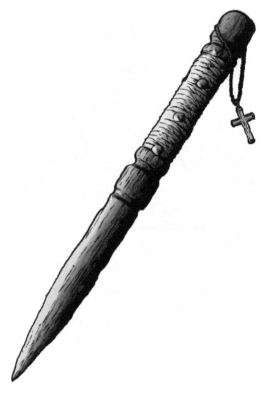

You're now getting close to finishing your
character. All that is left is to roll up your
starting pounds (£) and purchase weapons,
armor, and other items. Roll 2D6 to determine
your starting pounds. Weapons have a damage
rating and a cost (in £). £ replaces Gold in
this game, but the two are interchangeable.

Melee Weapons			Ranged Weapons		
Name	Dmg	G	Name	Dmg	G
Dagger	1	1£	Holy Cross	1	2£
Wooden Stake	1D3	2£	Holy Water Sprayer	1D3	3£
Hammer	1D3+1	3£	Flaming Cross	1D3+1	4£
Wooden Polearm	1D3+2	4£	Blessed Long Whip	1D6	5£
Steel Polearm	1D6	4£	Stake Crossbow	1D6+2	7£
Pollaxe	1D6+2	6£	Sacred Cross	1D2	3£
Billy Club	1	1£	Acid Vial	1D3	3£
Sharpened Cross	1D3	2£	Rusty Revolver	1D3+1	4£
Silver Dagger	1D3+1	3£	Silver Revolver	1D3+2	5£
Cane Sword	1D6	4£	Mini Stake Revolver	1D6+3	8£
Silver Sword	1D6+1	5£	Rifle	1D6+2	7£
Sickle	1D3+1	3£	Bladed Boomerang	1D3+2	5£
Rapier	1D6	4£	Black Powder Pistol	1D6+1	6£
Sythe	1D6+1	5£	Black Powder Rifle	1D6+2	7£

Section 10.0

Armor and Items

Armor grants the wearer a boost to their health, will, or both. Other items such as food and holy water can be used to restore lost health and will. All items are consumable. They can be used at any point in the game, even during battle. The number to the left of each item is used for Search Rolls after a battle is won.

Armor			Items		
Name	Bonus	G	(#) Name	Bonus	G
Shield	+3H	1£	(2) Bread Crust	1D3 H	1£
Top Hat	+3W	1£	(3) Wine	1D3 W	1£
Black Cloak	+6H	2£	(4) Steak Meal	1D6 H	2£
Chainmail	+6W	2£	(5) Holy Water	1D6 W	2£
Blessed Robes	+6HW	3£	(6) Miracle	FULL HW	6£

Section 11.0

Generating Rooms

Begin the game by choosing a random square on the graph paper and generating the first room in the dungeon (the **Dungeon Entrance**).

To generate a room, roll 2D6. The number rolled is the number of squares in the room. These can be drawn in any way, shape, or form so long as they are orthogonally connected.

Next, roll 1D3 (1D6 divided by 2 rounded up). This is the number of NEW doors added in the room (in addition to any door you just used). Draw small rectangles to represent the doors along any single square's edge to designate an exit. Each time you move through a door you will generate a new room in this manner. The **Dungeon Entrance** doesn't contain monsters.

In the following example, the player rolled 2 dice. One came up 6 and the other 4 for a total of 10. They then built a room of ten squares as so. Next, they rolled 1 die. The result was 6.

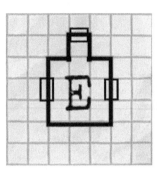

Divided in half that is 3. 3 doors. The player then drew in three smaller rectangles to designate where the doors in the room are located.

Finally, the player marks the first room with an E to show it is the Entrance/Exit of the dungeon. A player may backtrack any time to the Entrance if the dungeon gets too hard. However, they don't earn the extra bonus for killing the Boss!

Section 12.0

Doorways

When you leave the Dungeon Entrance (or any room in the dungeon once it has been cleared of monsters) you will choose 1 door in the room to move through. Before moving through, however, you will need to make a Door Roll. Roll 1D6 on the door chart provided in the scenario. Some scenarios will add new door results, but there are 4 absolute basic door options that could occur:

Unlocked: The door is unlocked and you may move through freely without stopping.

Stuck: The door appears to be stuck. Make a ST check to get through. If you fail you may lose 1 WILL to reroll and try again.

Locked: The door is locked. Make a WI check to pick the lock. If you fail you may lose 1 WILL to reroll and try again.

Trapped: The door has a trap attached to it. You must make a WI check to disarm it and move through. If you fail, take 1D3 damage but still move through.

Once a door has been moved through, shade the doorway in black to show that you no longer have to roll when using that door. (This just makes tracking easier)

If there are multiple doors in a room, you can choose to attempt one door. If you fail, you can choose a different one. Retrying any stuck or locked door always requires a Will loss. You MUST always make an attempt on a trapped door once you've rolled it up--as the trap catches you unawares as you are attempting to go through.

Section 13.0

Room Types

Each newly generated room you enter also has a Room Type that will make it slightly different from other rooms.

Upon entering a room, roll 1D6 on the scenario's Room Type chart. Each type will have a lettered code for you to write inside the room to remind you. Types include things like dirt or stone floors, water, or even crypts and tourture chambers.

Some rooms types only add flavor to the story, but most will either include a trap, an obstacle, or a die roll modifier (usually +1) for one stat that makes things harder for you.

In some scenarios, a room type might ask you to roll on an events chart for that room. This increases the possibilities within a single dungeon or scenario.

Section 14.0

Monsters

Every room has monsters. After Entering any room and determining its type roll 1D6 on the scenario's monster chart to generate the monsters in the room.

Roll once to determine the monster type. Roll a second time to determine the number of that monster that appears in the room. Each monster has a Max number that can appear in a room. Even if you roll higher, only the Max number will appear and no more can appear than the number of squares in a room. Monsters also have a Health Damage (H-DMG), Willpower Damage (W-DMG), and Life Force (LF).

Section 14.1

Vampires

The Hammer + Cross core rulebook focuses mainly on Vampires for enemies. All monsters you roll in the included mini-campaign will either be vampires or a minion controlled by a vampire.

Every vampire has two extra statistics in addition to the original set which all monsters have:

Bloodletting (BL): Each time the player rolls a 6 during a melee attack (an instant failure), the vampire bites them and drinks their blood. The BL is how much LF it regains.

Power (P): This is the mental strength of the vampire. It is the amount of faith the player will lose if they fail during the Faith check.

A vampire's minions, be they human or animal, won't have these abilities. They are simply servants of the damned, condemned to do evi's bidding blindly.

Section 15.0

Combat Procedure

The instant you run into any monsters, combat begins.

Combat in the Micro Chapbook RPG system is extremely simple and is completed in 3 easy steps.

1. **Bravery:** Check to see how brave you are.
2. **Ranged Combat:** If able, make a ranged attack against the monsters now.
3. **Melee Combat:** You MUST make a melee attack. Make a melee attack now.

Once all three steps are complete, start over from the top and repeat them all. Do this until all the monsters are defeated, you are killed, or you have elected to run away.

Section 16.0

Bravery

The sight of any monster, be it large or small, can invoke the deepest fear in even the bravest or vampire hunters. During the Bravery Step make a CH check. If you pass, gain 1 Willpower. If you fail, you lose Will according to the monster's W DMG (Usually you have to roll a die to see how much). If your Will ever reaches 0, all rolls take a +1 modifier to the die result as your character is losing hope in their ability to succeed in their quest. (A natural roll of 1 STILL always succeeds despite this or any other modifier. Will mods stack with room mods). Even if you have 0 Will, always make the Bravery Check to see if you earn a Will back.

Section 17.0

Ranged Combat

IF (and only if) the current room is 4 squares or larger you may make a ranged attack. To make a ranged attack you must have a ranged weapon. Roll a DE stat check. If you succeed at the check, apply weapon damage to the monster's Life Force. (usually by rolling). Extra damage after a monster is defeated CAN'T roll over to other monsters in the room. You targeted a single monster with the attack.

Section 18.0

Melee Combat

During Melee Combat you MUST make a melee attack using a ST check. If you succeed, apply the weapon's damage to the monster's LF. (usually by rolling). Similarly, damage can't roll over to multiple enemies. However, if you FAIL, one monster in the room deals damage to you. Roll the monster's H DMG and apply it to your health rating. If it reaches 0 you die.

Section 18.1

The Vampire's Bite

If you roll a natural 6 during melee combat AND your opponent is a vampire, the vampire bites you. The vampire will regain LF in the amount of it's Bloodletting rating.

Section 19.0

Running Away

After ALL steps of combat you can elect to run away by making a CH check. If you fail, one monster in the room deals damage and another round of combat begins. If you pass choose any door in the room to escape through. If it is a door you haven't explored yet roll on the Doorway chart. If it is stuck or locked and you fail the roll, one monster in the room deals damage and combat resumes. If you escape, add a number to the room and record what monsters were left behind on a sheet of paper. They will be there if you return.

Section 20.0

Faith Check

AFTER a room is cleared of monsters AND ONLY IF the player was bitten by a vampire during combat, that player must now make a Faith Check using their WI. If the player fails, they lose Faith in the amount of the vampire's power. The player may spend 1 Willpower to reroll this check as many times as they have Will to spend.

If their Faith ever reaches 0, they succumb to the powers of darkness and die, transforming into a vampire themselves.

Section 21.0

Search Rolls

After you have cleared a room of all monsters roll 1D6. If you get a one through five you earn that much in pounds. Add it to your money on the character sheet.

If you roll a six, roll on the Items chart in the section on armor and items. Each item is assigned a number (in parenthesis to the left of the item name on the item chart). If you roll that number you find that item. If you roll a 1 on the items chart you find nothing. Search rolls replace Treasure rolls in this version of the game system.

Section 22.0

The Boss

Each dungeon scenario has its own boss
(marked with a * on the Monster Chart) The boss
will not appear until you've encountered all
the other monsters on the chart at least once.
Additionally, the boss will only appear in
specific rooms, as designated by the scenario.
If you roll the boss when it can't appear,
reroll. Once it is defeated, the scenario ends.

Section 23.0

Backtracking

If the game gets too difficult at any point in the dungeon, or you are afraid you are nearing death and/or succumbing to vampirism, you may work your way backwards and return to rooms you already visited--including the Exit where you may voluntarily leave. If you ran away from a room, the monsters you left will still be there.

If you left the room empty, roll 1D6. On a roll of 6, new monsters appear. Roll for monsters as normal. Once you've defeated the monsters, make a Search Roll -2 to see if the monsters were carrying any. If the result is 0, you get no reward. You can't find items as the room has already been searched once.

Section 24.0

Leveling Up

After defeating a boss, count up the number of rooms you explored. Earn 1 pound for each room. If you did not defeat the boss, you don't get the bonus. In between scenarios you may spend 100 pounds to add +1 to one stat (50 for an easier game). No stat can be higher than 5. You may also buy new equipment. You may only have 1 melee and 1 ranged weapon at a time.

Section 25.0

Vengeance on Volkoria Village

Vengeance on Volkoria Village is a mini campaign for Hammer + Cross. It takes 1 player on a journey to the small rural Transylvania village of Volkoria. There, they will meet the frightened town's folk who believe a vampire is behind the current string of illness and death. The player will meet the skeptical Dr. Lorca who can join the player in the campaign as a companion. They will explore the village and the surrounding countryside, investigating for vampires.

Section 25.1

Volkoria Village

Volkoria Village is a small and rural Transylvania hamlet that has recently been plagued by strange deaths. The local mayor is under the impression that it is some sort of epidemic that is sweeping through the land.

The local priest, however, believes that there is something far more devilish and sinister going on. That's where you come in. You've been called upon to investigate the village by the priest.

On the next page you'll find a village map.

Volkoria Village

Below you'll find the numbered key to the village map (and the corresponding section here in the book). Each numbered location is a place you can visit. Some will involve speaking to a local. Some act as simple stopping points to recover or shop. Most, however, are "dungeon" scenarios where you will explore a randomly generated area and fight monsters. The end of each scenario will offer you more insight into the mystery (as well as a reward to assist in the campaign).

Village Map Key:
1. Raven's Caw Inn (25.3)
2. Mayor Windell's House (25.5)
3. The Church (25.6)
4. Town Mill (25.7)
5. Food Storage Barns (25.8)
6. The Blacksmith (25.9)
7. Home of Vincent Draper Family (25.10)
8. The Marsh (25.11)
9. Town Outpost (25.12)
10.   Black Woods (25.13)
11. The Caves (25.14)
12. Volkoria Castle

Section 25.2

Getting Started

The Story Thus Far: You recently received a letter from the priest of Volkoria imploring you to come to the village. He believes there are forces of evil at work which the Mayor refuses to do anything about.

Gameplay Basics: You will begin by visiting Location 1: The Raven's Caw Tavern. After that you can visit almost any location on the map you wish. Simply turn to the corresponding section for the area as listed and read the description.

The exception is that you may not visit the castle until you've visited the cave, the cave until you've visited the woods, and the woods until you've visited the outpost.

You are never obligated to finish a dungeon in one go. If things get too hard or desperate for you, you can backtrack to the exit and come back to try it again another time. You can choose to keep the layout of the dungeon from a previous run, but repopulate rooms you've already visited with new monsters OR start a new layout on a new piece of graph paper. It's up to you.

You don't get the campaign rewards listed at the end of a dungeon until you've fully beaten the dungeon boss.

You may also always return to a dungeon in the town and run through it again for more money/rewards. During a subsequent runthrough you can, similarly, keep the layout from before or start a new layout. However, you don't earn the campaign rewards for that dungeon a second time.

Finally, you can play any dungeon here in the campaign as a stand alone "one-shot" game.

Section 25.3

1: Raven's Caw Inn

Arriving in the town one foggy and late afternoon, you ride up the west path in your carriage past the wet marsh and straight to the largest building at the center of town. You promptly climb out and pay the driver who seems nervous. Upon receiving payment, he throws down your luggage without any regard for your belongings. With that, he zooms off back into the fog.

Picking up your bags, you head into the cramped inn. People sit at tables around the room with drafts of ale and wine. An old man slurps soup in the corner. There is a somber tone in the air and no one seems to be talking. Your presence goes mostly unnoticed, except by the woman behind the bar. She is an attractive woman of around 25 with ruby red lips and raven hair. "Evening, stranger. How can I help you?" she asks. "We have food and drink available and rooms for the night."

You take a seat at the bar.

If you ask about the local priest, read section A.

If you ask about the mayor, read section B.

If you ask about the "plague," read section C.

If you choose to use the Inn's services you can:
> Rest for 1 pound to completely heal your health and willpower.
> Purchase a Bread Crust, Wine, or Stake Meal.

You can use these services at any point in between dungeons when you revisit the Inn.

λ – The Priest: You ask her if she can direct you to the local priest. She tells you that he lives in the rectory attached to church. "He is a nice guy, but a little eccentric," she admits. "He seems to believe there are demons or vampires here in town." She laughs it off. She tells you the church is inside the stone wall section of town to the northwest. "Unfortunately, they close that portion down at night and it is already getting dark. You might still be able to make it if you hurry."

If you ask about the walled in section of the town, read section D.

B – **The Mayor:** You ask her if she can tell you about the local mayor. She tells you that he lives in the mayor's manor. "No one knows him that well," she admits. "He seems to spend all day hidden away in that manor house." She tells you the manor is inside the stone wall section of town to the northwest. "Unfortunately, they close that portion down at night and it is already getting dark. You might still be able to make it if you hurry."

If you ask about the walled in section of the town, read section D.

C – The Plague: You ask her about the current plague that seems to be effecting everyone. She is about to answer when a handsome tall man interrupts her. "I can answer that," he declares. Standing up from a nearby table where he is having lunch with a young female companion, he walks across the room. Sitting on the stool next to yours, he introduces himself. "I am Dr. Henry Lorca. That young woman over there is my assistant, Ms. Graves. We are here at the mayor's request to investigate the illness." He proceeds to inform you that the pandemic seems to be a blood disease. The victims of it become anemic and eventually grow weak and die. "I'm still trying to pinpoint the source cause," he tells you. "The most recent victim is a young woman, the daughter of Vincent Draper--the local blacksmith."

He asks you who you are. You inform him you've been sent for by the priest. The doctor seems unimpressed. "There is nothing here but science. Any old foolish superstition won't help these people," he insists.

You disagree, claiming that yesterday's superstition is today's science. He shakes his head in disappointment. "Just you wait. Once I find the source of this disease and stop it in its tracks, you'll look the fool."

You realize he is challenging you.

If you try to persuade him that you should work together, make a CH check. If you pass, you may bring Dr. Lorca and his assistant with you as companions in any dungeons.
If you decide you are better off working without him. Simply send him on his merry way with a wave of your hand.

Once per visit to the inn (in between dungeons), you may try to convince the doctor to join you again. If you fail, you have to wait until the next visit to try again.

⬦ – The Town Wall: You ask the woman about the town wall to the northwest. She informs you that both the mayor and priest lock the gates on the area at night. They only began doing this recently as the gate used to be open all the time. However, she believes the men and their families fear the plague and have therefore been keeping themselves locked away.

The old man in the corner throws a spoonful of his soup on the wood floor. "They ain't afraid of no disease or devil. Just us poor folks. They only built the damn wall to show who had the money and who didn't."

"Don't mind him," the barmaid whispers. "He's lived in this town longer than anyone and is unhappy with the new mayor."

"Mark my words," the old man says, standing up, "those rich folks will get what is coming to them. With that, he marches out.

Section 25.4

Dr. Lorca and Ms. Graves

Doctor Henry Lorca is a man of science. He doesn't believe in vampires or the supernatural--at least not yet. If you successfully convince him to work together with you, he and Ms. Graves can become your companions for the game.

Companions and Doors: When encountering a door in a dungeon that requires a check, you may choose a companion to attempt it. If they fail they may try again or you may switch to yourself or another companion. If it is a door trap, only that character takes damage.

Companions and Rooms: For room types, ALL party members are affected by the room's modifiers. If it is a room trap or Stat check, ALL party members must make the check.

Companions and Combat: During combat, companions act the same as your main character. They make the same Bravery Check. They may make ranged and melee attacks during those respective game steps. They take enemy damage when they miss, etc. You may choose which order to have your characters attack in each turn.

Companions and Leveling Up: Companions level up in the same manner as your main character.

Companions and Dying: Once a companion reaches 0 Health. They are dead and out of the game.

Companions and Vampirism: If a companion becomes a vampire, you will immediately have to fight them. They are a Vampire Fledgling for purposes of the game.

You will find the character sheets for both the doctor and his assistant on the following pages.

Hammer✝Cross

Character Record Sheet

Name: Dr. Lorca **Order:** Sun **Class:** Doctor

STATS

2	1	2	3
St	De	Wi	Ch

Proficiency: Wits

WEAPONS

Ranged: Silver Revolver **Melee:** Cane Sword

ARMOR   ITEMS

Top Hat
Black Cloak

WILL   HEALTH   FAITH   £

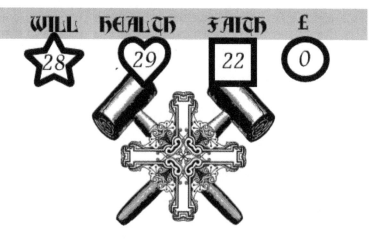

28   29   22   0

58

Hammer✝Cross

Character Record Sheet

Name: Ms. Grave **Order:** Dagger **Class:** Nurse

STATS

1	4	2	1
St	De	Wi	Ch

Proficiency: Wits

WEAPONS

Ranged: Black Pow Pistol **Melee:** Silver Dagger

ARMOR   ITEMS

Black Cloak   Ale

WILL	HEALTH	FAITH	£
23	31	22	0

Section 25.5

(2) Mayor's Manor House

You pass the large gates of the stone wall which separates the richer portion of the village from the poor. Thankfully, those gates haven't been closed for the night yet-- despite the moon rising in the sky.

In the distance, you can see the Mayor's large and elaborate manor house sitting back on a hill. Approaching the manor house you notice it has its own high wrought iron fence with spikes along the top.

You find the front gate to the fenced in manor gardens padlocked. It seems the mayor has already locked himself inside. You may make a ST check +1 to break the lock. If you fail, you may spend 1 willpower to try again, and may do this multiple times.

Alternatively, you may also attempt to climb the fence with a DE roll. If you pass, you still take 1D3 damage, cutting yourself on the spikes in the climb over. If you fail, you take 1D6 damage from the climb and fall down outside the fence. You may spend a willpower to attempt this again and may attempt multiple times, always taking damage as directed.

Finally, you can choose to wait to enter until you have a Manor Key in your possession.

Once you have made it past the fence, you head for the front door and knock. When no one immediately answers, you call out. Still, there is no answer. This time, you push open the door and step inside the dark interior.

Generate your first room. Mark the room with an E. This is the Entrance Hallway to this "Dungeon."

Manor Doorways		
5-6	Unlocked	Move through freely.
3-4	Stuck	ST Check
2	Locked	WI Check
1	Stairs	Move to a new level.

Stairs will take you to a new floor of the manor house. Either upstairs or the basement. While on the main floor decide where the staircase leads and mark it with either an up arrow (upstairs) or a down arrow (downstairs). When entering a new floor for the first time, create a new room randomly on a seperate sheet of graph paper. When returning to a floor, you will either choose 1 pre existing staircase (any) to come out on OR start a new room in any open space available.

While upstairs, every staircase leads downstairs to the main floor. While in the basement every staircase leads upstairs to the main floor. Each floor has its own room types. Rooms on separate floors can't connect except by stairs. You begin on the main floor

Main Floor Room Types

1	Hallway	H	An empty hallway. No effect.
2	Dining Room	D	You always find 1 bread crust after completing this room.
3	Kitchen	K	You always find 1 steak meal after completing this room.
4	Lounge	L	This room is comfortable. You can sit down for a moment to recover 1D3 health.
5	Study	S	Books of all sorts fill the room. −1 WI rolls in this room
6	Powder Room	P	You look in the mirror and swear you don't recognize the face staring back. Make a WI roll or lose 1 WI.

Second Floor Room Types			
1	Hallway	H	An empty hallway. No effect.
2	Nursery	N	A strange sound of a baby crying seems to come out of nowhere. Make a WI roll or lose 1D3 Willpower
3	Bedroom	B	A lot of fancy personal belongings sit on the dresser. Money earned is doubled in this room.
4	Master Bedroom	M	There appears to be a pile of dead bodies on the bed. Make a WI check or lose 1D6 Willpower.
5	Storage	S	Lots of boxes block the way. +1 on all DE rolls.
6	Restroom	R	Blood appears to run from the faucets. +1 WI rolls in this room.

Basement Room Types			
1	**Hallway**	**H**	An empty hallway. No effect.
2	**Dirt**	**D**	A dirt floor. No effect.
3	**Storage**	**S**	Lots of boxes block the way. +1 on all DE rolls.
4	**Wine Cellar**	**W**	Every time you beat this room, find 1 wine.
5	**Root Cellar**	**R**	It is extremely dark down here. Add +1 to DE and ST rolls.
6	**Coffin**	**C**	There is a coffin in this room. Make a CH check to find the bravery to open it. If you succeed, you find the ghoul and get 1 free attack before combat begins. If not, treat the room as normal and spawn monsters.

Manor Monsters				
#	Monster	Max	H-DMG	W-DMG	LF
1	Jerusalem Cricket	6	1	1	1
2	Spider Swarm	5	1	1D2	1
3	Rat Nest	5	1	1D3	2
4	Bat	4	1D2	1D3+1	3
5	Black Cat	3	1D3	1D3	4
6	Ghoul*	1	1D3+1	1D3+1	5

*The Ghoul will only appear in a basement room. The ghoul is not a vampire and therefore doesn't have the vampiric traits.

Campaign Reward: After defeating the ghoul, you find the mayor's body shoved into a wooden box. His throat is cut. It seems the ghoul desired to be a vampire. Unfortunately, ghouls are just poor souls who are bitten by a vampire but don't lose enough blood to die. The weak willed ones go insane for lust of blood. A second look reveals the ghoul was likely the old man from the inn. You also find the mayor's will, which leaves his money to "whomever is with him at the end." Earn 1D6x5 pounds.

Section 25.6

(3) The Church

You pass the large gates of the stone wall which separates the richer portion of the village from the poor. Thankfully, those gates which haven't been closed for the night yet--despite the moon rising in the sky. The church is a large stone building sitting snugly in a corner against the high wall. Saying a small prayer, you enter.

Passing through the foyer you move into the cavernous chapel. High vaulted ceilings can barely be illuminated by the hanging wall lanterns and candle lit chandelier. Magnificent stained glass windows depict the life of Christ on the right side of the church as well as the seven circles of hell on the left.

Approaching the front of the chapel, you spot someone kneeling at the altar and praying. You instantly realize it is the priest. Reverently, you kneel beside him and cross yourself.

Seeing you, his eyes grow wide. "Thank goodness you're here," he gasps, gripping you by the shoulders. "Things are far worse than when I wrote." He informs you that more and more of the town's women are falling ill. The worst? A nun who was on assignment here at the church has vanished and he has reason to believe that the fiend—a vampire—has managed to somehow penetrate the church's defenses.

You suggest an immediate search of the building. The two of you work together, combing the building for any clues. Make a WI check to search.

If you fail the search roll, you promise the priest you'll return to search again another time but will investigate other portions of town first. You may leave and come back later or spend 1 Willpower to roll again.

If you pass, you find an old cellar door in the rectory. The door sits ajar. The priest informs you this leads to the crypts beneath the church. He can go no further with you for fear of the dark. You may begin the dungeon by rolling the entrance to the crypts.

(You may always purchase Holy Water and Miracles at the church.)

Crypt Doorways		
5-6	Open	You may generate the next room by peeking inside. Then you can choose to enter or not.
3-4	Unlocked	Move through freely.
1-2	Stuck	ST Check

Crypt Room Types			
1	**Dirt**	**D**	A dirt floor. No effect.
2	**Preparation Room**	**P**	This room has embalming tools, a bloody table, and empty coffins. Anything could be hiding. +1 CH rolls.
3	**Storage**	**S**	Lots of boxes block the way. +1 on all DE rolls.
4	**Water**	**W**	This part of the crypt has flooded. +1 on ST rolls.
5	**Antechamber**	**A**	This side room has coffins laid into slots in the walls. Add +1 to the # of Monsters in the room.
6	**Altar**	**T**	A basin filled with old water sits at the center of this room. Make a WI check as you drink from it. **PASS:** Gain 1D3 Health and Willpower **FAIL:** Lose 1D3 Health and Willpower

Crypt Monsters					
#	Monster	Max	H-DMG	W-DMG	LF
1	Jerusalem Cricket	6	1	1	1
2	Spider Swarm	5	1	1D2	1
3	Rat Nest	5	1	1D3	2
4	Vampire Bat	4	1D3	1D3+1	3
5	Black Cat	3	1D3	1D3	4
6	Fledgling Vampire*	1	1D3+1	1D3+1	5

*The Fledgling Vampire is the boss of this dungeon. She only appears in the Altar room. Once defeated, read the Campaign Rewards section. Additionally, the Fledgling Vampire has the following vampiric stats:

Fledgling Vampire	Bloodletting	Power
	1	1

Campaign Reward: You find the nun, Sister Mary, sitting in the corner. "Thank you," she says, "but I could have handled him eventually." You find her boasting and confidence odd for a nun, but like it. She reveals that the fledgling vampire was the daughter of the local miller. The parents will need to be informed.

Sister Mary also mentions how the vampire gave some details on where she came from. Seems she was out walking near the marsh when she was attacked and changed into a vampire. The next day, the town thought the girl was missing and sent out a search party for her. That next night, the new vampire went and saw her best friend, the daughter of Vincent Draper. Sister Mary now fears that the young Draper girl is also infected with vampirism. She wishes she could do more to help. Make a CH check to invite her along. If you pass you now have the option of adding Sister Mary to your party. Your party may have up to 3 people (the lead character and 2 companions) at a time. If you failed, you may return to the church later to try again.

Hammer✠Cross

Character Record Sheet

Name: Sis. Mary   **Order:** Cross   **Class:** Nun

STATS

St	De	Wi	Ch
1	1	3	3

Proficiency: Charisma

WEAPONS

Ranged: Sacred Cross   **Melee:** Dagger

ARMOR	ITEMS
Blessed Robes	Bread Crust Holy Water x2

WILL	HEALTH	FAITH	£
32	28	28	0

Section 25.7

(4) The Mill

The old town mill appears run down, like it hasn't been properly used in months. Weeds and grass sprout up all around it. The propeller only creaks lazily back and forth in the wind. The player can search three different areas:

If you visit The Barn read section A

If you visit The Farmhouse read section B

If you visit The Windmill read section C

ⴷ – The Barn: The barn door is locked and chained closed. You may make a WI check +1 to attempt to open it. If you fail, you may spend willpower to try again. OR if you have the Iron Key you may enter.

Inside the barn you find stacks of long wooden boxes. They appear freshly made as if waiting for a customer to pick them up. You fear they are coffins awaiting new vampires.

B – **The Farmhouse:** This small hut of a home has a single room. Things lay in disarray, as if the miller and his family left in a hurry. Two pots of half eaten gruel sit atop the table. A pot with dried gruel sits on the counter.

You may make a WI check to search the room. If you pass, you find an old brass key under a rug, and 1D6 pounds.

C – The Windmill: The door to the Windmill is stuck. You must make a ST check to push it open. You may spend willpower to reroll. Once inside the cramped space, you notice a trap door in the floor. The door has a small brass lock on it. You may make a WI check to pick it, spending Willpower to reroll. If you have the brass key you can enter without rolling. The trap door leads to a grain storage cellar beneath. The cellar is a mini dungeon with only half the room types and monsters.

Cellar Doorways		
4-6	**Unlocked**	Move through freely.
1-3	**Stuck**	ST Check

Cellar Room Types		
1-2	**Dirt**	D	A dirt floor. No effect.
3-4	**Storage**	S	Lots of boxes and bags of grain block the way. +1 on all DE rolls.
5-6	**Burrow**	B	Some sort of animal has burrowed down into this room, making its home here. This room automatically has Fanged Opossums in it.

Cellar Monsters

#	Monster	Max	H-DMG	W-DMG	LF
1-3	Fanged Opossum	6	1D3	1	1
4-5	Black Cat	3	1D3	1D3	4
6	Fledgling Vampire*	2	1D3+1	1D3+1	5

*The Fledgling Vampire(s) are the boss of this mini dungeon and there will always be 2 of them when they appear. They can appear in any room. Once defeated, read the Campaign Rewards section. Additionally, the Fledgling Vampire has the following vampiric stats:

Fledgling Vampire	Bloodletting	Power
	1	1

Campaign Rewards: The Fledgling Vampires you killed are revealed to be the Miller and his Wife. You earn 2D6 pounds.

Section 25.8

(5) Food Storage Barns

Two old rotting barns sit near the edge of town. Supposedly, this is where the emergency food rations are kept if anything happens in town. However, these barns don't look kept up. The player can explore the two barns.

If you enter Barn 1 read section A.

If you enter Barn 2 read section B.

λ – Barn 1: Stepping inside the barn, you grimace at the strange scent of rotting food. Clearly, no one was keeping an eye on this storage. Flies buzz around the bags of grain and vegetables. Worms crawl in and out, turning your stomach. You want to turn away and leave.

If you choose to stay and search the place, make a CH check. If you fail, you turn away, unable to stand the stench. You may spend willpower to try again. If you pass, you are able to search and find a key to the Mayor's Manor gate. What was it doing here?

As you stand to turn toward the door to leave, you face a strange figure framed by moonlight through the barn's slatted wood walls. It has labored breathing and a jaw that hangs askew. You must kill it to get out.

#	Monster	Max	H–DMG	W–DMG	LF
–	Rotting Zombie	–	1D3	1	4

Reward: You step back from the corpse, wondering if it was some poor hungry soul who tried to eat the food and became cursed. You find a gold necklace on it worth 10£

B – **Barn 2:** This barn seems surprisingly empty. No food stored up as you originally supposed.

Make a WI check +1 to search the barn. If you fail, you feel that there is nothing of interest here and leave. If you pass, you find a loose board along one of the walls and pull it off. It reveals a strange rolled up piece of yellow paper. Unrolling it, you find that it is a **Map of Volkoria Castle**. This will come in handy later.

Just as you stand to leave, you hear a low growl from behind one of the stalls. You turn just in time to see a wolf with eyes aglow like two yellow fires glaring at you. It lunges at you.

#	Monster	Max	H-DMG	W-DMG	LF
–	Wolf Guard	–	1D6	1D3	5

Reward: The furry body slumps over with one last whine, the beast defeated. You may keep the pealy worth 4₤

Section 25.9

(6) The Blacksmith

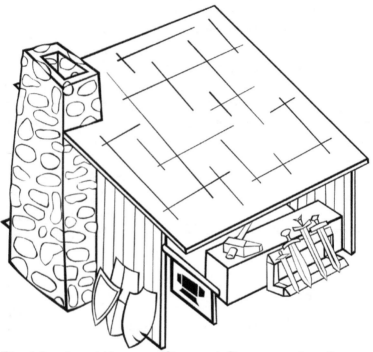

The blacksmith, one Vincent Draper, stands over an anvil with a red hot piece of steel which he is hammering. He sweats and has a pale expression of exhaustion about him. "What can I do for you?" He asks. He refuses to speak about the illness going around.

You may purchase weapons and armor here.

Section 25.10

(7) The Vincent Draper Family Home

This small local home belongs to the blacksmith, Vincent Draper, and his family. Rumor in town is that this family's daughter is the latest victim of the "plague." As you approach the door and knock, you hear footsteps shuffle inside. A moment later a woman appears, only opening the door enough to let in a crack of light. She appears disheveled with hair in all directions, dark circles under her eyes, and pale skin. "Yes?" she inquires. "Can I help you?"

You inform her you are here to see the daughter's symptoms. The mother seems reluctant. Make a CH check to convince her to

let you in. If you fail you may spend willpower to try again.

If you pass, she lets you in. The house is cozy, if a little cluttered. Clearly these people have been preoccupied with their daughter's sudden illness.

"My husband isn't here right now," the woman informs you. "He is working at the blacksmith shop. He is spending more and more time there. It's his way of dealing with this problem, I suppose," she sighs, motioning for you to follow her up a narrow staircase to the second floor. At the first bedroom near the front side of the house, you step inside and see the young afflicted woman laying on the bed.

Her breathing seems labored, her skin is ghost white, and she looks to be on death's doorstep.

"We just don't know what else to do," the mother whispers, standing off to the side. You request to examine her, but the girl seems reluctant. Make a CH check to calm her. If you fail, you may spend willpower to reroll.

If you pass, make a WI check to examine her more closely.

If you pass, you find the two small puncture wounds on the next. Also, the pale weakness, the clear loss of blood, all of it points to a

vampire attack. More than that, you find the girl clutching some sort of amulet. A **crest of the sun.** She gives it to you, whispering, "This will help. Please save me." Thanking the girl, you inform the mother to hang garlic over all the windows in the house and around the bed. Also, bless the home with holy water at all entrances. The mother is confused, but agrees.

If you fail the examination check, you can find no real reason for her illness. While you believe it is a vampire, you have no hard evidence. You only hope you can save the girl.

Section 25.11

(8) The Marsh

You've heard rumors and clues about The Marsh in town. Some believe night creatures walk the land at night. Some of the local teens have vanished while exploring the marsh.

You hope to find some more clues here. Raised paths of dirt cross through the wet portions of the land and the trees. You will have to carefully navigate them.

When mapping outdoor dungeons, there is an added element to creating "rooms" (or better known as clearings in this instance). Each time you generate a new room, and after rolling the doors (called paths in this instance), the area directly around it must be shaded in to show the local foliage--all adjacent squares except the ones leading to "doors" (or exits) are shaded. In the marsh, you might use a grey or blue colored pencil to show the wet portions of the land. In a forest, you might use green.

In the example above, you can see how a player might roll through 8 areas of the map. Each has shading around it. However, you are free to build rooms directly adjacent to pre drawn shading--so long as there is at least 1 row of shading between areas where exits aren't connecting them.

Marsh Pathways (Doors)		
5-6	Open	You may generate the next room by peeking inside. Then you can choose to enter or not.
4	Blocked	Brambles and vines block the way. Make a ST check to cut them down.
3	Wet	A deep puddle separates the two areas. Make a DE check to jump across or take 1D3 damage.
2	Mud	Thick sticky mud makes up the path between these areas. You must make a ST check or get stuck. If you get stuck, lose 1 willpower and try again.
1	Sinkhole	This exit has a tricky bit of mud that is actually a sinkhole. Make a DE check to avoid it or get sucked in taking 1D6 damage.

Marsh Clearing (Room) Types		
1	Wood W d	This area has wooden planks over the ground for extra protection. −1 on DE rolls.
2	Dirt D	A dirt area. No effect.
3	Mud M	This sticky mud makes it hard to maneuver. +1 on DE rolls.
4	Water W	This part of the marsh has flooded. +1 on ST rolls.
5	Pit P	A large pit is covered by weeds here. Make a WI check to see it. If you fail, take 1D3 damage as you fall in. You must make a DE check to climb out. You may use willpower to reroll.
6	Overgrowth O	This area is rampant with weeds and brambles. At the end of each round of combat, you take a chance of scratching yourself on the brambles. Make a DE check or take 1 damage.

Marsh Monsters					
#	Monster	Max	H-DMG	W-DMG	LF
1	Snake	6	1	1D2	1
2	Bat	4	1D2	1D3+1	3
3	Rotting Zombie	3	1D3	1	4
4	Hungry Wolf	3	1D3	1D3	4
5	Wolf Guard	1	1D6	1D3	5
6	Acolyte Vampire*	1	1D6	1D3+1	7

*The Acolyte Vampire is the boss of this dungeon. It will only appear in a pit or overgrowth area. Once defeated, read the Campaign Rewards section. Additionally, the Vampire has the following vampiric stats:

Acolyte Vampire	Bloodletting	Power
	1D2	1

Campaign Reward: You earn 2D6x2 pounds, found in a chest near the vampire's coffin. This vampire doesn't appear to be a former town person, but a servant to a greater vampire.

Section 25.12

(9) Town Outpost

Approaching the Town Outpost, the only gateway into the nearby woods, a soldier looks down upon you. "Who goes there?" he calls out. "No one past this point. The woods are too dangerous."

You try to explain that you are attempting to hunt an evil demon known as a vampire. He doesn't believe you and asks for proof.

Make a CH check plus +5 to the die roll. Also subtract the modifiers below from the roll for each one that applies. If you pass the check, you successfully convince him that there really is a vampire just beyond the woods. You may now move freely from town to the woods. If you fail, he sends you away. You will have to try again later.

CH Modifiers	
Sister Mary is in the party	−1
Dr. Lorca is in the party	−1
Crest of the Sun is in your inventory	−1
Map of Volkoria Castle is in your inventory	−1
Acolyte Vampire killed	−2
X3 Fledgling Vampires killed	−3

Section 25.13

(10) The Black Woods

The Black Woods. The dark a foreboding mass of trees just to the north of town. Those villagers who believe in vampires are deathly afraid of this place. They believe that the vampires are out there somewhere and are hunting.

Even those who don't believe in vampires are afraid. They think whatever illness is sweeping through the village is somehow connected to the woods.

Either way, don't let your guard down.

When mapping outdoor dungeons, there is an added element to creating "rooms" (or better known as clearings in this instance). Each time you generate a new room, and after rolling the doors (better known as paths in this instance), the area directly around it must be shaded in to show the local foliage--all adjacent squares except the ones leading to "doors" (or exits) are shaded. In the marsh, you might use a grey or blue colored pencil to show the wet portions of the land. In a forest, you might use green.

In the example above, you can see how a player might roll through 8 areas of the map. Each has shading around it. However, you are free to build rooms directly adjacent to pre drawn shading--so long as there is at least 1 row of shading between areas where exits aren't connecting them.

Woods Pathways (Doors)		
5-6	Open	You may generate the next room by peeking inside. Then you can choose to enter or not.
4	Blocked	Brambles and vines block the way. Make a ST check to cut them down.
3	River	A small running river separates the two areas. Make a DE check to jump across or take 1D3 damage.
2	Spike Trap	A shoddy wooden spike trap waits to impale you. Make a WI check to disarm it or take 1D3 damage.
1	Mystic Door	A strange and ethereal portal resides here. Make a WI check to move through it. If you fail, you end up back at the entrance

Woods Clearing (Room) Types		
1	Wood	**W**	This area has wooden planks over the ground for extra protection. −1 on DE rolls.
2	Dirt	**D**	A dirt area. No effect.
3	Mud	**M**	This sticky mud makes it hard to maneuver. +1 on DE rolls.
4	Lake	**L**	This area has a small lake. +1 on ST rolls.
5	Pit	**P**	A large pit is covered by branches here. Make a WI check to see it. If you fail, take 1D3 damage as you fall in. You must make a DE check to climb out. You may use willpower to reroll.
6	Overgrowth	**O**	This area is rampant with weeds and brambles. At the end of each round of combat, you take a chance of scratching yourself on the brambles. Make a DE check or take 1 damage.

Woods Monsters					
#	Monster	Max	H-DMG	W-DMG	LF
1	Vampire Bat	4	1D3	1D3+1	3
2	Rotting Zombie	4	1D3	1	4
3	Wolf Guard	4	1D6	1D3	5
4	Fledgling Vampire	3	1D3+1	1D3+1	5
5	Acolyte Vampire	2	1D6	1D3+1	7
6	Vampire Bride*	1	1D6	1D6	10

*The Vampire Bride is the boss of this
dungeon. It will only appear in a lake or
overgrowth area. Once defeated, read the
Campaign Rewards section. Additionally, the
Vampires have the following vampiric stats:

	Bloodletting	Power
Fledgling Vampire	1	1
Acolyte Vampire	1D2	1
Vampire Bride	1D3	1D2

Campaign Reward: There appears to be far more
vampires than you expected. Roll on the items
chart 5 times.

Section 25.14

(11) The Caves

The Caves at the edge of the woods appears to be the only route to make it up to the castle-- the place you believe the Master Vampire to be hiding at.

However, getting close also means more danger. Your stomach ties itself in knots as you think about what may lay beyond. More servants of the damned? More powerful vampires?

There is only one way to find out.

Cave Doorways		
5-6	Open	You may generate the next room by peeking inside. Then you can choose to enter or not.
3-4	Blocked	Boulders and stones block the way. Make a ST check to move them out of the way.
2	Portcullis	Someone has installed a portcullis that blocks the way to the next part of the cave. You must make a WI +1 check to open it.
1	Spike Trap	A steel spike trap waits to impale you. Make a WI check to disarm it or take 1D6 damage.

Cave Room Types			
1	**Dirt**	D	A dirt area. No effect.
2	**Stone**	S	A stone area. No effect.
3	**Ice**	I	The deeper you get into the cave the chillier it becomes. This room even has ice all over the floor, making movement difficult. +1 on DE rolls.
4	**Lake**	L	This area has a small underground lake. +1 on ST rolls.
5	**Pit**	P	A large pit lays before you in the dark. Make a DE check to jump over it. If you fail, take 1D3 damage as you fall in. You must make a DE check to climb out. You may use willpower to reroll.
6	**Chapel**	C	You enter a room that appears to be a makeshift chapel of sorts. However, the crosses are all upside down. There is no worship of anything holy here. The horror of this place wears on your soul. +1 on CH rolls.

Cave Monsters					
#	Monster	Max	H-DMG	W-DMG	LF
1	Ghoul	4	1D3+1	1D3+1	5
2	Wolf Guard	4	1D6	1D3	5
3	Fledgling Vampire	3	1D3+1	1D3+1	5
4	Acolyte Vampire	3	1D6	1D3+1	7
5	Vampire Bride	3	1D6	1D6	10
6	Vampire Lord*	1	1D6+1	1D6+1	15

*The Vampire Lord is the boss of this dungeon. It will only appear in a Pit or Chapel. Additionally, if you have the Crest of the Sun in your possession, all your attacks are made at −1 against the Lord. Once defeated, read the Campaign Rewards section. Additionally, the Vampires have the following vampiric stats:

	Bloodletting	Power
Fledgling Vampire	1	1
Acolyte Vampire	1D2	1
Vampire Bride	1D3	1D2
Vampire Lord	1D6	1D3

Campaign Reward: Vanquishing the Vampire Lord, you lay back in the dirt to take a break cleaning the blood from your hands. The most horrifying thing of all? You know this wasn't the strongest vampire you must face. The Master Vampire is still out there. He is the one that must die to save the town.

Getting up, you find a path leading out into the open air and moonlight. A mountain stream trickles nearby and you kneel to drink. You feel rejuvenated from it and heal all your health and willpower. Filling a vial with the water, you take it with you. (This is the equivalent of a Miracle from the items chart). You may return to refill your vial at any time. You may not have more than the one vial.

Standing up, you look up the mountain path toward your final destination. The great castle looms dark and monstrous against the moonlit sky.

Section 25.15

(12) Volkoria Castle

Volkoria Castle. Once inhabited by the Lord of this land. Seemingly abandoned, it now is the home of evil. It seems some Master Vampire along with his clan of children, servants, and minions have all moved in and made their home here. It was a perfect place, after all, so near a food source.

Crossing the large stone bridge to the front gate, you look up and realize just how large the place is. You pray you'll be able to find the vampire in the labyrinth.

Castle Doorways		
6	Open	You may generate the next room by peeking inside. Then you can choose to enter or not.
5	Unlocked	Move through freely.
4	Stuck	ST Check
3	Locked	WI Check
2	Portcullis	A portcullis blocks the way. You must make a WI +1 check to open it.
1	Stairs	Move to a new level.

Stairs: The vampire's castle has 5 levels to it.

Towers
2nd Story
* Main Floor *
Basement
Catacombs

You will need a seperate sheet of paper for each level. Each new stairs result will take you to a new floor of the castle. Stairs can only lead up or down to a connecting floor (as outlined in the table on the previous page. When generating a stairway, draw an up arrow (upstairs) or a down arrow (downstairs) to show which direction it leads. The Catacombs may only ever lead up to the Basement. The Towers may only ever lead down to the 2nd Story.

When entering a new floor for the first time, create a new room randomly on a seperate sheet of graph paper. When returning to a floor, you will always choose 1 pre existing staircase to come out on OR generate a new room in any open space on the floor.

Each floor has its own room types. Rooms on separate floors can't connect except by stairs. <u>You begin on the Main Floor.</u>

Castle Map: If you have the map of the castle in your possession, you may generate any room before choosing to enter it. (This does not include seeing which monsters are in there).

Towers Room Types		
1	Hallway	H	An empty hallway. No effect.
2	Storage	S	Lots of boxes block the way. +1 on all DE rolls.
3	Torture Chamber	T	Strange devices take up this room. Make a WI check so not to get trapped in one. If you fail take 1D3 damage.
4	Coffins	C	A bunch of old coffins lay in this room in a circle, a sleeping place for new vampires in training. +1 on CH rolls.
5	Altar	A	Some sort of demonic altar sits at the center of the room. Make a WI check or lose 1D6 willpower.
6	Widow's Walk	W	This is a dangerous area to be with a steep drop. Make a DE check or fall off taking 1D6 damage and ending up in a random Main Floor room.

Second Story Room Types		
1	**Hallway** H	An empty hallway. No effect.
2	**Nursery** N	A strange sound of a baby crying seems to come out of nowhere. Make a WI roll or lose 1D3 Willpower
3	**Bedroom** B	A lot of fancy personal belongings sit on the dresser. Money earned is doubled in this room.
4	**Master Bedroom** M	There appears to be a pile of dead bodies on the bed. Make a WI check or lose 1D6 Willpower.
5	**Storage** S	Lots of boxes block the way. +1 on all DE rolls.
6	**Restroom** R	Blood appears to run from the faucets. +1 WI rolls in this room.

Main Floor Room Types			
1	Hallway	H	An empty hallway. No effect.
2	Dining Room	D	You always find 1 bread crust after completing this room.
3	Kitchen	K	You always find 1 steak meal after completing this room.
4	Library	L	Books of all sorts fill the room. -1 WI rolls in this room
5	Courtyard	C	The light of the moon feels refreshing on your face. Heal 1D3 health.
6	Stables	S	Strange horses of and blackest black stare at you with red eyes. Make a WI roll or lose 1D3 Will.

Basement Room Types			
1	Hallway	H	An empty hallway. No effect.
2	Dirt	D	A dirt floor. No effect.
3	Storage	S	Lots of boxes block the way. +1 on all DE rolls.
4	Wine Cellar	W	Every time you beat this room, find 1 wine.
5	Root Cellar	R	It is extremely dark down here. Add +1 to DE and ST rolls.
6	Coffin	C	There is a coffin in this room. Make a CH check to find the bravery to open it. If you succeed, you find the ghoul and get 1 free attack before combat begins. If not, treat the room as normal and spawn monsters.

Catacombs Room Types		
1	**Dirt** D	A dirt floor. No effect.
2	**Preparation Room** P	This room has embalming tools, a bloody table, and empty coffins. Anything could be hiding. +1 CH rolls.
3	**Storage** S	Lots of boxes block the way. +1 on all DE rolls.
4	**Water** W	This part of the catacombs has flooded. +1 on ST rolls.
5	**Antechamber** A	This side room has coffins laid into slots in the walls. Add +1 to the Monster # roll.
6	**Altar** T	A basin filled with old water sits at the center of this room. Make a WI check as you drink from it. **PASS:** Gain 1D3 Health and Willpower **FAIL:** Lose 1D3 Health and Willpower

Castle Monsters					
#	Monster	Max	H-DMG	W-DMG	LF
1	Wolf Guard	5	1D6	1D3	5
2	Fledgling Vampire	4	1D3+1	1D3+1	5
3	Acolyte Vampire	4	1D6	1D3+1	7
4	Vampire Bride	3	1D6	1D6	10
5	Vampire Lord	1	1D6+1	1D6+1	15
6	Master Vampire	1	2D6	2D6	25

*The Master Vampire is the boss of this dungeon. It will only appear in a Tower or Catacombs level. Additionally, if you have the Crest of the Sun in your possession, all your attacks are made at −1 against the Master. Once defeated, read the Campaign Rewards section.

Additionally, the Vampires have the following vampiric stats:

	Bloodletting	Power
Fledgling Vampire	1	1
Acolyte Vampire	1D2	1
Vampire Bride	1D3	1D2
Vampire Lord	1D6	1D3
Master Vampire	2D6	1D6

Campaign Reward: As the Master Vampire turns to ash and blows away with the wind, you breathe a sigh of relief. As you head out of the castle into the morning, the sun is shining. You want to smile but somehow can't knowing all the lives already lost. You do, however, feel some peace at knowing you've saved souls in the process. Heading back into town, you are welcomed with open arms. Anyone who had been stricken sick is now better. A celebration is held in your honor with all manner of food, deserts, mead, and music.

You automatically level up two Skill areas of your choosing.

Section 26.0

Playing With a Game Master

The Game Master in this game is called the
Lord of Night (or LN for short) Using the
following tips, play the game in a
traditional manner with a Lord of the Night
controlling the monsters and telling the
story.

The LN can choose to prebuild the
dungeon beforehand, choosing what is

in each room, the layout, the doors, the traps, where the Boss is hiding, and more.

The LN can add in treasure chests with set money or items inside.

The Mini-Campaign can be run like an ordinary RPG adventure with more embellished and detailed Non-Player Characters and story description by the LN.

The LN may choose to create their own story or campaign for players.

The LN may choose to run the game in a more "roleplay" style with added story elements, non-player characters, quest goals, etc.

In this way, the LN can use WI for all reading, writing, and intelligence based rolls. The LN may also use CH for all social based rolls with NPCs, enemies, and more.

Try playing the game on a traditional grid based game mat with miniatures. Each miniature can move 1-2 squares at a time orthogonally as part of the melee attack phase.

Ranged attacks may be made at a distance. Melee attacks may be made while adjacent.

Come up with your own house rules!

Section 27.0

Combining With Other Micro Chapbooks

This game is completely compatible with other products in the Micro Chapbook line with a few modifications:

Faith: Faith is a special element that is only used in the Hammer+Cross version of the system. It will not come into play in other scenarios or modules. Similarly, vampire powers are only used in this version of the game system. If you wish to use a character from another game in this one, give them a Faith rating.

Pounds: The currency of pounds can be equally exchanged for gold in the other versions of the game. Play this game with a character from another game and it will collect gold as normal. Play with a Vampire Hunter from this game in one of the others and they will continue to collect pounds.

Orders: Character Orders replace race in this game. You can feel free to take a class from another game and assign them an order. OR you can even take one of the classes from this game and assign them a fantasy race.

Hammer✝Cross

Character Record Sheet

Name: **Order:**   **Class:**

STATS

St   De   Wi   Ch

Proficiency:

WEAPONS

Ranged: **Melee:**

ARMOR   ITEMS

WILL   HEALTH   FAITH   £

Expand Your Adventure With These Stand Alone Micro Chapbook RPGs!

Find More World Building Options and Create Stronger Characters with these Micro Chapbook Supplements!

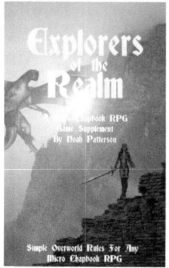